Resurrection Lily

Resurrection Lily

A Poetry Chapbook

by

Angela Hoffman

© 2022 Angela Hoffman. All rights reserved.
This material may not be reproduced in any form, published,
reprinted, recorded, performed, broadcast,
rewritten or redistributed without
the explicit permission of Angela Hoffman.
All such actions are strictly prohibited by law.

Cover design by Shay Culligan
Cover art by S. Tsuchiya via Unsplash

ISBN: 978-1-63980-221-0

Kelsay Books
502 South 1040 East, A-119
American Fork, Utah 84003
Kelsaybooks.com

For Emily and Natalie

*We have two lives, and the second begins
when we realize we only have one.*
—Confucius

Contents

Resurrection Lily	9
The Promised Land	10
Marbles	11
Homeless	12
The Exit	13
For the Homebodies	14
Hearty Tomato	15
Olly Olly Oxen Free	16
Live in Color	17
Play the Cards Dealt	18
Nothing Stands Alone	20
Sparrow Grass	21
Will-O-the-Wisp	22
Love Walks Precariously	23
If You Don't Heal	24
Fed, One Crumb at a Time	25
That Kind of Love	26
She Jumped	27
When in Flight, Geese Are Called a Skein	28
Descend	29
Shifting Delights	30
I'm the Twilight	32
Broken Birds Gather	33
The Fold	34
Merry-Go-Round	35
Love Is a Shovel	36
Envy Is the Tongue	37
A Plain Yellow Pumpkin	
Can Become a Golden Carriage	38
The Moon Tapped on Her Window	39
The Fall	40
Good and Evil	41
Headstand	42
Your Courage	43
Time to Take Off Winter's Coat	44

Resurrection Lily

The bulbs were given to me with the instructions to bury them
be patient with them, maybe even be surprised by them.
I was told to hold onto what might be, the possibilities.
Since it was the relative of the onion, I had no expectation.
In spring, thick stalks with bladelike leaves emerged, two feet tall
only to die back mid-summer, their foliage signaling their end.

Later that summer, in the same spot
I noticed leafless stalks, naked ladies
had popped up unexpectedly, and days later, magically
pale pink clusters of lily-like flowers showed up fully
bearing vulnerability, beauty on the ends of their unadorned stalks.
Second chances, a rebirth of possibilities.

The Promised Land

If the land remembers the stories
carried with the people crossing the Jordan River
does the dirt remember the cuss word I scribbled with the stick
beneath my bedroom window, a room I should have been safe in?
Does the ice remember the scrape of my skates
dreaming of a better tomorrow?
Does the grass remember my fingers digging for acorns
later bloodied from the nail that pierced them
stringing them into a necklace, to win the love of my mother?
Does the road of my childhood home still hear my voice
talking out loud on my lonely walks to no place?
Does the sidewalk remember my middle-school awkwardness
giving in to kisses, lost in wanting to be loved by anyone?

Stuck in the wilderness, ending up going nowhere
other than where I started
I fall to my knees, put my head to the ground, listen
for the remembered stories of how to get to the promised land.

Marbles

Knuckles in the dirt, you flicked your thumb
to get your marble into the hollowed-out hole.
If successful, you were considered poisonous.
Hitting another marble now, meant it was yours for the taking.

Most of mine were eventually lost in this game of keeps.
I began watching from the sidelines
hoarding what I had left in my leather drawstring bag, envious
of the crystals, boulders, and steelies my friends collected.

My life has been a bit like that; a collection of hits
pieces of me, stolen.
Over time, I resorted to observing from the outside
wishing I was better, had more, was of value.

I'm ready to trade in my cat-eyes that just watch
get down on my knees in the dirt, dump out my bag
let my life roll where it will, taking all necessary risks.
I'm just not playing for keeps.

Homeless

Moving about on surface-level streets, empty, void
I stick close to home, yet feel homeless
not sure where I belong, fearful of the unknown.
Lonely, I hunger for humanity.
No one notices, stops, looks me in the eye.

I turn around, take the dark passage underground
sit, listen to the rumble of my mind's wheels
until the rhythm soothes, lulls.
I need not do anything. It is done to me.
Someone looks me in the eye.
I realize I am not sitting alone.
No longer homeless, I can venture far.

The Exit

I know not if I am driving to or from in this blinding snow
but it is dark and I have miles to go, so
I head out on Straight Road
my destination, Damascus. I've been on this road before
familiar like this dream. I pass the old homestead
the church I once belonged to, the liquor store, and more.
I know up ahead, on the far north side
there will be an exit sign, the one I miss every time
considering it too late, all I want to leave behind
all my unanswered prayers.

And then, headlights. I skid, spin, but make the exit
travel downhill, until I come to a stop.
I get out, open the trunk, empty all it holds
by the side of the road: empty promises, untruths
my settling, my smallness, my emptiness
my greed, my envy, my jealousy, my still voice, my anxieties
my lack of courage, my lack of worth, my inability to love
my every last thorn.
I'm an expert at boasting my weaknesses, *lest I become too elated.*
I will take the high road from here on out
for there is no fall so deep that grace cannot lift.
Why didn't you just tell me
the exit was the answer to my prayers?

For the Homebodies

I want to say something wonderful for the homebodies;
those content in being unadventurous.
For them, the path leading home is worn thin
finding it even in the dark.
They are willing to embody their bodies
content in the skin of their homes.

Solitariness being their forever friend, never betrays or abandons.
There is no conforming, cowering, compromising
no showing up for something someone else deemed necessary.

That's why I want to say something beautiful
like, our hearts are tender.
We are butterflies, chrysalises off
floating freely with our guards down
sticking around, comforted by what we have created.

We are Dorothy, clicking our ruby slippers together
longing for a return to familial doings, familiarity
realizing that all we need resides inside, not out there.

In the simple, safe, be-yourself-space
by a crackling fire with a book
in a room with paints and journals
in the garden picking strawberries
on the porch with family, no words necessary
we find solace. Non-pretentious, we are enough.

Hearty Tomato

The tomato I hold in my hands is far from perfect.
Not all of it ripened evenly. Parts are green, soft, firm.
It has scarring, a black spot. It has split open a bit.

If only someone would cup my heart
run their fingers over my scars, the broken-open, bruised parts
soft parts, hard parts
see the part not ripe, still child-like
the part ripened a bit too far, the blossom rot
notice its beat so faint
bring it back to a hearty *thump-thump, thump-thump.*

Olly Olly Oxen Free

First, I was *It*. God went hiding.
I closed my eyes and counted
looked in all the wrong places.
He was not in my unanswered prayers
not in the pews at church, nor in a box of doctrines.
I looked outside in vain.
I eventually had to call out, *Olly olly oxen free*

and then God was *It*. I went hiding.
He had to come find me.
I hid in sacks of loneliness, in closets full of secrets
under a bed of betrayal, in a heap of lies
under piles of regret. I stayed still and silent, kept myself small.
He always found me.

I learned over time his hiding places.
I found him in the garden, by water
on hiking trails, in the quiet morning
buried in the layers of another's pain.
One of his favorite places was inside
as close as my breath.
I know if I can't find him, I need only call out
Olly olly oxen free, and He will come find me.

Live in Color

I live in gray. I've forgotten how to live in color.
Remind me how to see the leaven and light in my life:
the earth swaddled in gull-white snow
the sky a watercolor wash at sunrise, sunset
the dance of the sun like a kaleidoscope
the apricot lips of a kiss
the iridescent side of my foe
pink joy against black pain
wheat and weed shades all mixed
shadows of suffering mingled with translucent joy
a sea of skin tones coexisting
yellow laughter, rainbow celebrations
the hard transparent truth, the depth of emotion
home's golden hues.

Play the Cards Dealt

365 days await, the sum of the cards, plus a joker or 2
depending upon the leap.
52 weeks, cards to be played in the right or wrong way.
It all depends.
12 months, 12 court cards.
Jack, queen, king, 3 months in each season show face.
There will be warm red days and cold black nights.
Accept them all.

4 seasons follow suit:
spring of childhood, struggles to find joy, our church of beliefs
hearts on fire
summers of youth, our plantings deep in the earth
the work of peasantry with clubs
autumns of growth, vocations, wealth of creations
diamonds in the air
winters of knowledge, waters of old age
highest ranking warriors with spades.

13 cards in each suit, 13 lunar cycles of waxing and waning
waiting for you to show up full as Wolf, Snow, Worm, Pink
Flower, Strawberry, Buck, Sturgeon, Corn, Hunter, Beaver, Cold
every once in a while, Blue.

A day worth an ace of desire, deuce of union, or pips of faith
satisfaction, change, adjustment, victory, power, new beginning
success, depending upon the draw.
Perhaps you'll get a one-eyed jack of heart or spade, all wild
even be king or queen for a day.

Face down, face up, you will have to face being
buried, cut, dealt, shuffled, flipped
stacked, discarded, marked, ranked, forced.

You might bluff, exchange, fold, follow, go out, lead, pass, renege
trick, turn, ante up, smear, run, unload, partner-up, win.
Play the cards dealt or make your own rules.

Nothing Stands Alone

Do you remember the dell in the valley
the farmer who took his wife
the child, nurse, cow, dog, cat, rat
all choosing another
until the cheese stood alone in the middle?

I played that game all wrong.
The cheese was never the loser.
I missed seeing the circle, hands embraced
the choosing of those on the outside
the community, the epiphany, bowing before the mystery
inside, in the center, chosen, never alone.

Sparrow Grass

With the pandemic, so many at home
everyone took to gardening, it seems.
When I went to purchase my asparagus crowns
all I found were empty bins.
I resorted to planting servant seeds in the trenches I had dug.
I had no real expectation for them.

But soon I saw frail stems poking their way
offering a scrap of hope.
They continued to grow and by fall were feathery, tall.
I checked on them this winter day.
They had turned brown, bowed down
just as we had in this, our second winter.
I dream of the spring

when the arrows of sparrow grass will resurrect
thick with scales, green
after their time in the trenches.
I'm told they will need a third winter
until they are ready for harvest.

Will-O-the-Wisp

The decay of time, things lost, the past
bodies burdened, dreams dead, goals gone—
all things decomposed will combust into gas.

Luring us with their mysterious glow
with longing, we linger
long on marshy bogs
chasing the will-o-the-wisp
like fluorescent blue fireflies
on the darkest of nights
willing to be mired down, led astray
for a chance to catch the real, the impossible
resurrect ourselves back to life.

Love Walks Precariously

Having lost trust, I sought solid ground
protected places, shallow waters, smooth sailing
spaces low and flat
everything accounted for, under control
by me, for you
with the word love tagged to it all.

I've learned love involves precarious acts
thin ice, high places, risky edges
touch and go situations
loose footings, holdings unstable
constant calls for courage
from inside, outside, all sides
no safety nets, no one managing the moves
just open waters, wide spaces
assuring one is still alive
with just a bit of prayer on the side.

If You Don't Heal

If you don't heal what hurt you
you'll bleed on people who didn't cut you.
If I don't lift that lid, climb into death's box
lie down next to you, mother of my mother
hold you tight until I crack you open, until you tell me your story
I'll hold onto my stories I patched together
from the little I know about you
marrying a man your father's age
being cold and cruel to my mother
drinking yourself to death at such a young age
your open wounds infecting all those near you.

Your self-loathing lingers and lacerates the bones of your lineage
along with our need to numb, forget. Fear drives our every move.
We keep small in the balm of our own boxed-in worlds.

Tell me then about your dreams that were dashed
your glories and gashes, your passions and piercings
your secrets and scars, your loves and longings
your beliefs and bruises, your talents and scrapes
every mystical moment and every dark hurt.
Hold nothing back, mother of my mother.
Tear off your shroud, attend, mend, minister the salve
restore and renew.
If you heal what hurt you
you'll bless the people who didn't cut you.

Let's stitch new stories with heroines healed
brave and beautiful, confident and caring.
Let's leave our wounds, fears, tears in your tomb.
I will return to the living, while you finally rest in heaven.

Fed, One Crumb at a Time

In the early morning dark
the purr of my cat on my lap, reading by lamplight
putting thoughts into words, words into anchors
I promised to give up resisting, the knots of doubt
loneliness, being against the world.

I'll lean forward, towards, like the sunflower.
I'll take the rope let down, eat the bread from my pocket
look for delights.

I'll accept inefficiency, spontaneity
linger at single-tasks, not multi-task
one crumb at a time.

That Kind of Love

I know nothing of *that* kind of love any more.
The one where bodies ache
for the touch of the other
lips on neck, hands cupping face
fingers reaching, bodies spooning
arms embracing, trust holding
eyes that search a room, linger, light up.

I know of the hard-scrapped, hard-fought kind
filled with failings, trying harder, starting over
again, promises made, not always kept
the steadying of the boat, the capsizing
the responsible, duty-bound kind
with hard persistence that wears thin
having been stretched so many times
wondering if it will hold.

She Jumped

Like a peony bud so firm, that opens
or a poppy head that lifts to the sun
the beautiful lift their heads high with shoulders back
white smiles on full display, assuredness in full bloom.
Their beauty comes naturally.
Even if she didn't wear a speck of makeup, she'd still be gorgeous.
We are not one of the lucky ones, I was told.

And so, I set to work. Long story short, that troublesome thistle
would never become a flower.

Now my skin sags in the most visible of places.
My eyelids have disappeared, my lips have gone thin.
Children find it fascinating to trace the veins on my hands
like obscure roads on a map, point out that extra fold on my neck.
I slouch, my eyebrows are sparse prickles on the margins.
My skin is speckled like a sparrow egg.
My smile does not come naturally. I work at that too.

I work at trying to figure out what beauty even means
try on various kinds:
Beauty is only skin deep. Beauty is in the eye of the beholder.
I never asked you to be her; I asked you to be you.
Beauty arrives when you finally decide to be yourself.
A thistle has a crown that provides nectar.

The headline this week: *USA Miss America Jumps to Her Death*

When in Flight, Geese Are Called a Skein

After two long years
self-isolation taking its toll
I long to belong
be with others with a bit of their heart
knit from the same skein as mine;
sorrow tangled with hope.
I need someone to hold
one or the other.

Held in holy formation, accounted for, seen
I'd grab for delight
falling back when I tire
part of one flock, geese in flight.

Descend

beneath the skin
under the dung heap
in deep waters
below deck
underground
in the hole, agape
where surely something holy is buried.

Nothing happens on the surface
or with tentative waiting.
Dig with all you have.
Pull life from all the stubborn places.
Even Christ came down.

Shifting Delights

No matter the season, time was expansive
wide open, abundant
filled with softness, slowness.
Even boredom was celebrated.
The days of youth were spent outdoors
rooted in holy ground, wonderment in the

return of the robin, rhubarb
pastures of buttercups
mudpies and cow pies
endless nights under moonlight
fireflies, cloudless skies
monarchs, milkweed wishes
troves of acorns, hickory nuts
maple leaves to bury in, piles of burning brush
paths forged through tall grasses, precarious houses in trees
first snowfall, ponds scraped in eights by skates
steep hills for sleds, drifts of shrouded silence
angels and men of snow

time rolled with ease
following nature's lead
seasons marked only by shifting delights
which over time
became wasted time
measured time
scarce, against the time
ticking on the clock

piles of responsibilities, return of insecurities
clouds of worries, steep bills
jobs forged, precarious children
troves of events, sleepless nights
paths lost, hearts scraped
shrouds of silence, buried in life

But angels and gods, slow to mention who they might be
disguised as our life, never leave
so, I wait, now closer to the end, for the return of the robin.

I'm the Twilight

Something else arose, I did not intend
upon the white paper, now marked blue.
There was no coaxing, encouragement on my part.

Everything's a fine line between the sacred and the profane
between darkness and light; twilight, dusk.
I'm stuck in the teeter.

I am a seismograph, sensitive to every subtle shift in mood.
I'm awkward standing on that fine line
between arrival and departure, longing and eluding
healing and breaking, standing for or giving in
receiving or taking, opening or closing.

They said I was shy, but if I was sad, I kept silent.
If I was giddy, I kept a straight face, in case.
I was blue as the green that gave away its yellow
the dark that pulled the shades, slipped on its slippers.

Broken Birds Gather

Your centeredness, grounded-ness in something more
is alluring. I long to meet you, get to know you better
yet I already know you—
a part of you is in me, a part of me is in you.

I've watched you like a hawk, learned your ways
flew under your wings, spread by faith.
Becoming undefended, I tried on beloved-ness.
Experiencing unitedness, I appear to fly solo
but you are still there, a relationship
found, bound in desire.

By attraction, rather than promotion
more broken birds are gathering
wondering if there is a better way to fly.

The Fold

I struggle with the fitted sheet, messy, twisted, bunched
never tidy like the tight folds of the top sheet
I'm able to get right.
We are made for delights, overspilling, spilled over
more longing, more allowing, no enclosure holding.

I stop my wrestling, trying to control the corners, rest.
Perfection no longer matters. Something happens in between
the folding, unfolding, and being gathered into The Fold.

Merry-Go-Round

The merry-go-round in the park of my childhood
is gone now, declared too dangerous.
I would grab hold of the metal bar and begin running.
Eventually I would jump on, sit down, knees drawn up.

Then another child would show up, take control
grab the bar and run, making it spin
faster
and faster.
It was then that I tried moving to the center.
It was safer there, but eventually the force would pull me back
to the edges.

At times I was left hanging on, my body dragging on the ground.
The scrapes and bruises were not enough
to keep me from getting on again. I stayed there day after day
year after year. I'll get off now.

I'm tired of ending up in the same place
exhausted from all the gripping, watching life pass by.
I've been to the center enough times, protected, held in place.
I feel brave enough to give the swings a go.
There I can fly.

Love Is a Shovel

If *hope is the thing with feathers*
that perches in the soul
love is the shovel that will unbury that bird.

Love loosens the soul of the soil
breaks apart the hard clods of clay
digs up old bones, sometimes finds ones
you didn't even know were buried there.

Digging deep is never easy.
It involves looking into the recesses of the dark
seeing past it, forgiving.
At times, it becomes too much to bear.
You cover over what you discovered
sometimes even yourself.

If you are persistent, you will find treasure
sea glass, bits of foundation, gold
yourself, the other, the One
and that bird.

When you do, cup that bird ever so gently.
The shovel will stand at the ready.

Envy Is the Tongue

They leave behind breadcrumbs.
Hungry, craving fullness, I watch, follow
pocket what I can.
It's not their stuff or their opportunities I desire.
I don't covet their careers or their clothes.

My tongue, salivating for a taste
attempts to ask about their bounty
but remains heavy, silent, shameful in its wanting.

I just want a bite of their bravery
a chunk of their confidence
a heaping of honesty
more delight, less disappointment
more grace, less grief
not more of the same
a morsel of trust
a scrap of significance
a piece of purpose
my share of strong relationships
a helping that will fill the hole in my heart
a belonging to the one body of bread.

A Plain Yellow Pumpkin
Can Become a Golden Carriage

I picked the squash from my garden
split it open, buttered, baked it.
Disguised in the restraints of its skin
it looked perfect on the outside, appropriate in its attire.
Inside, it had no taste, yet disappointed
I ate with devotion

filling up on logic, reason, seriousness, all things rational
believing in sensible rules and what sensible people say.
Guilted, shamed for wanting more of a taste
I stuck to the bland bites

but longed to be unreasonable, impossible, crazy, a fool
throw my food, leave it there on the plate
let go of out of season beliefs.

I wanted to be filled with passion, taste aliveness
not just fill up with the expected, the ordinary, the tasteless.
Plain yellow squashes *can* become impossible hopes
for the zanies.

The Moon Tapped on Her Window

Sometimes I show up waning, cratered by life
or I go missing on the dark side.
Eclipsed, all alone, I see things through the shadows
of the story I created that I am just a sliver.

Other times I show up on the bright side
full, embodied, remembering to look for the stars;
those souls that help me to be brave enough to come out.
I remind myself that I am never-not full
that I have the strength to move even the ocean.

The Fall

The green vestments of ordinary time are laid to rest.
Elaborate reds reserved for feasts now adorn, for it is harvest time.
We toast with cabernets, merlots, pinot grigios
walk the multi-colored cloaked path
through the rain of tissue paper yellows against a Payne's gray sky
hearing the swishing and wishing of whispered prayers.
The young try to rouse the fallen as they run through
sending them flying.
There is a chill in pain's gray and the golden sun deceives
shining on the veined leaves that wrinkle, dry, die
before they are shrouded with a funeral pall of white.
Buried and sealed, they will be reborn to green.

Good and Evil

. . . and all was good.
Eve, woman of breath
took the blame, shame
for getting it right
choosing to be free
choosing to have a choice.
She took a bite.
Naked and vulnerable
with only her apple skins
she recognized her original goodness
fashioned in God's image.

Adam, man of dirt
gave patriarchal justification for his ruling
over her for her choosing
not recognizing human nature
never desires the bad fruit.
He hid behind the tree of masculinity
choosing strength over a gentle core.

In my original goodness
I'll choose my fruits
not the ones handed to me
sometimes bruised, rotten, unripe.

Headstand

Enough of being sure-footed, sensible.
I want to learn to stand on my head
turn the world upside down
see with new eyes
learn a different way of being
have first-hand knowledge from the bottom up.

I'd walk the talk with my mouth on the ground
put myself closer to walking in your shoes
maybe even recognize You.
I'd develop tenacity, not giving up at each fall
let everything that really matters
settle deep down into my soul.

Your Courage

Wren, you sit on the birch branch
causing good trouble
drowning out all falsehoods with your noise
awakening the souls around you
who sense an importance with no time to waste.
Your song of truth to the blue sky
does not match your perceived smallness.
Let it all be the same for me.

Time to Take Off Winter's Coat

There is such a thing as too much patience, too much tolerance
when the whisper becomes the shout
when the knot in the rope begins to slip.

Songbirds at dawn trick us into rising earlier than planned.
Tulips poke their heads into the congregation of dead leaves.
Robins return despite the cold reception they receive.
Daylight lingers longer as clocks are set ahead.

It is later now than before in the arc of my life.
I'm caught in the place between dusk and night
unwilling to risk, planning ahead, staying in place
I am among those leaves.

I must live in the space between dawn and day
where life emerges, unplanned, brave
accepting the life waiting for me
emerging distances I never dreamed.

About the Author

Angela Hoffman lives in Wisconsin. Her poetry has appeared in *Solitary Plover,* Wisconsin Fellowship of Poets' *Museletter* and *Calendar, Agape Review*, *Verse-Virtual, Visual Verse,* and *Your Daily Poem.* She committed to writing a poem a day during the pandemic. Spirituality and nature often inspire her poetry.